So
of the
Coqui

A Puerto Rican folktale
adapted by Julia Wall
Illustrated by Brad Ramsey

Characters

Boa
Wind
Lizard
Giant Toad
Queen Parrot
Tree Frog

Lizard, Boa, Giant Toad, and Tree Frog: Zzzz!

Wind: Hello, Queen Parrot.

Queen Parrot: Wind, I'm so glad to see you have blown into Puerto Rico. Please tell me, from the Wind's point of view, do my subjects appear chubby and idle?

Wind: Beautiful Queen Parrot, I'm afraid the animals of Puerto Rico appear to be somewhat overweight and under-exercised.

Giant Toad: Did you hear that, fellow animals? Our Queen Parrot and Wind think we are fat and lazy.

Lizard: They can call us what they like, Giant Toad. I'm done with tree climbing. I'm going to waddle under some ferns and spread out in the shade. Do you want to join me, Boa? Under your own fern, that is.

Boa: Lizard, I remember a time when you were slim and full of energy. But hey, I can't talk... my waist is as thick as a tree trunk. All I do these days is eat and sleep. A shady fern does sound **appealing**.

Giant Toad: Boa, you think you've got problems. Look at me. I'm as big as a bull!

Tree Frog: At least you can still see your toes, and giant toads are supposed to be large. I can't hop or climb as a tree frog's meant to do because my belly's so round. I have to roll from place to place!

Lizard: No darting about for me. I'm too **weary**.

Boa: No slithering about for me. I'm too sleepy.

Giant Toad: No jumping about for me. I'm too tired.

Tree Frog: No leaping about for me. It's nap time.

Lizard, Boa, Giant Toad, and Tree Frog: Zzzz!

Queen Parrot: What a racket! I can't hear myself think. I shall have to do something about the snoozing state of these animals. There's no work being done on this island. They're always resting!

Wind: I suggest we leave the animals to their nap, for now. Come fly with me to the other islands and we'll see what the animals there are doing.

Queen Parrot: Ahh, I see lizards dancing...

Wind: ...and look, there are snakes slithering about like lightning...

Queen Parrot: ...and frogs hopping in **humungous** leaps. I think I'll pass a law that all the animals of Puerto Rico must go on a diet. I'll make gym membership compulsory and I'll limit sleep to the hours of darkness.

Wind: My friend, it might not be that easy.

Queen Parrot: Then *what* can I do to make the animals get fit?

Wind: Queen Parrot, I believe I may have the answer.

Queen Parrot: I'm listening.

Wind: If you hold a race, then your animals will have to exercise in order to be **competitive**.

Queen Parrot: Wind, the animals on my island are so large they can hardly move, let alone run! There's no way they'd want to enter a race.

Wind: They will if you offer them a special prize.

Queen Parrot: Mmm, it'll have to be a *very* special prize to tempt these lumps of lard off their barrel-like behinds... but it's worth a try!

Wind: I agree, Queen Parrot.

Queen Parrot: Royal subjects, I hereby announce that in one month's time a race will be held. The winner will receive a very special, secret prize.

Lizard: I wonder what it will be!

Boa: I hope it's a takeaway bar so I don't have to waste energy constricting every meal.

Giant Toad: I want a bigger mud hole. I've outgrown mine.

Tree Frog: That will only appeal to toads, Giant Toad. The ideal prize for me would be to be able to sing 24 hours a day.

Boa: One thing's for sure – we're going to have to get fit for the race.

Lizard: These push-ups are hard work! I'd nearly forgotten how to flick my tail, stick out my tongue, and inflate my **dewlap**.

Boa: I'm actually enjoying being able to slither again. I'm getting slimmer by the day.

Giant Toad: Mud hole exercise is the best! My jumps are improving all the time.

Tree Frog: Exercise and practise all you like, friends, but I plan to win the race!

Giant Toad: You tree frogs are dreamers. You don't stand a chance, Tree Frog.

Tree Frog: Just you wait and see, Giant Toad. I have a plan.

Queen Parrot: Well animals, you can stop exercising now. The month is up. The race is about to begin. On your marks! Get set! Go!

Lizard: So long, slitherers, jumpers, and leapers! I'm going to dart to the finish line and win this race. Hey! Where'd that tree frog spring from?

Tree Frog: A flick of your tail won't bother us, I mean, me, Lizard!

Boa: Where did you come from, little guy? I'll sort this one out, Lizard!

Tree Frog: A **swat** from you won't bother me, Boa.

Giant Toad: Tree Frog is everywhere. I'll whack him out of the way.

Tree Frog: Ha ha! The finish line's just ahead. I've nearly won.

Lizard: Your race is about to end, little tree frog. I'm going to flick you out of the way, just like I did to your friends.

Tree Frog: No you're not, because I'm going to jump over the finish line. Here I go! Weeeee! I've made it! I've won!

Queen Parrot: Congratulations, Tree Frog. You're the winner!

Lizard: No he's not! The tree frogs cheated! There was more than one of them in the race. I should be the winner.

Boa: No, you shouldn't. You cheated too, Lizard! You flicked the **opposition** out of the way.

Giant Toad: You cheated as well, Boa. You swatted the opposition out of the way.

Tree Frog: And you did too, Giant Toad. You whacked the opposition out of the way!

Queen Parrot: Right, that's it. You used to be a bunch of fat layabouts, and now you're a bunch of thin cheats. I'm not so sure there should be a prize.

Tree Frog, Lizard, Boa, and Giant Toad:
Hey! That's not fair!

Wind: I have a suggestion, Queen Parrot. I'd like to recommend that the prize goes to the tree frogs, for working together to win the race.

Queen Parrot: Very well. Tree frogs, you shall be granted the ability to sing.

Lizard, Boa, and Giant Toad: But they *did* cheat.

Wind: That's true and because they did not win honestly, they shall only be able to sing at night, and they must stay on the island. If they leave this island, they shall die.

Lizard: This is why you'll only ever hear the tree frogs singing during darkness.

Boa: The sound they make, "Co-kee!" "Co-kee!" is what gives them their name, the coqui.

Giant Toad: And this is also why the coqui is only found in Puerto Rico.